Persian Food

An Easy Persian Cookbook for Cooking Classical Persian Food

By
BookSumo Press

Published by
http://www.booksumo.com

Table of Contents

Persian
Orange and Bean Stew

Prep Time: 12 mins
Total Time: 52 mins

Servings per Recipe: 4
Calories	493.2
Fat	6.5g
Cholesterol	0.0mg
Sodium	2222.4mg
Carbohydrates	85.6g
Protein	26.1g

Ingredients

1 tbsp olive oil
2 onions, chopped
3 cloves garlic, chopped
1 tsp salt
1 tsp cumin
1/4 tsp cinnamon
1 C. orange juice

1 lime, juice of
1 can tomato paste
4 (15 1/2 oz.) cans kidney beans, rinsed and drained
1 jalapeno, chopped
pita bread

Directions

1. Place a large skillet over medium heat. Heat the oil in it. Add the onion and cook it for 6 min.
2. Stir in the spices and cook them for another 6 min. Add the orange and lime juice. Cook them until they start boiling. Cook them for 12 min over low heat.
3. Stir in the peppers with beans. Cook them for 22 min. cook them for 5 min. serve your stew warm.
4. Enjoy.

PERSIAN
Potato Rice Stew

Prep Time: 3 hrs
Total Time: 3 hrs 45 mins

Servings per Recipe: 6

Calories	499.7
Fat	9.7g
Cholesterol	0.0mg
Sodium	11.4mg
Carbohydrates	92.5g
Protein	8.7g

Ingredients

3 C. of white long grain rice
4 tbsp cooking oil
3 - 4 medium potatoes

4 oz. water
salt

Directions

1. Get a large bowl: Place in it the rice and cover it with hot water and a pinch of salt. Place it aside.
2. Remove the peel of the potato and slice them.
3. Place a medium pot and fill half of it with water. Place in it the rice and cook it until it starts boiling. Once the rice is half done drain it.
4. Place a large pot over medium heat. Heat the oil in it. Stir in the water. Spread the potato in the pot and sprinkle on it some sat. Top it with rice.
5. Make a hole in the center of the rice layer and another 4 holes on the side. Drizzle some water on top. Put on the lid and cook them for 3 min over high heat.
6. Lower the heat and drizzle some oil top. Lower the heat to medium heat and cook it for 16 min.
7. Lower the heat to medium low. Drizzle more of some oil on top then cook it for 12 min. serve your potato rice warm.
8. Enjoy.

Persian
Nutty Rice

🍲 Prep Time: 10 mins

🕐 Total Time: 35 mins

Servings per Recipe: 4
Calories	280.1
Fat	9.7g
Cholesterol	15.2mg
Sodium	373.5mg
Carbohydrates	44.2g
Protein	5.2g

Ingredients

2 tbsp butter
1 C. white basmati rice, rinsed under cold
water in a fine mesh sieve
1/2 tsp salt
1/4 tsp cracked black pepper
1 garlic clove, minced
orange peel

1/2 tsp ground cinnamon
1/4 tsp curry powder
2 C. water
3 tbsp roasted pistachios
3 tbsp golden raisins

Directions

1. Place a large skillet over medium heat. Stir in it the rice for 5 min while stirring it.
2. Add the salt, pepper, garlic, orange peel, cinnamon and curry powder. Cook them for 2 min. Stir in the water and put on the lid. Lower the heat.
3. Cook them for 26 min. Place the cover aside and add to it the pistachios and golden raisins. Discard the orange peel. Serve your nutty rice warm.
4. Enjoy.

PERSIAN
Pistachios and Bean Pilaf

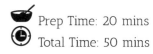

Prep Time: 20 mins
Total Time: 50 mins

Servings per Recipe: 4
Calories   411.0
Fat   15.6g
Cholesterol   0.0mg
Sodium   215.8mg
Carbohydrates   56.2g
Protein   15.4g

Ingredients

150 g frozen broad beans
1 tbsp olive oil
1 large kumara, peeled, cut into 2cm cubes (orange sweet potato)
1 brown onion, finely chopped
2 tsp finely grated ginger
1 tsp ground cumin
1 tsp ground coriander
1 tsp ground turmeric
1 tsp ground paprika

190 g quinoa, rinsed, drained
500 ml vegetable stock
1 bunch kale, stems trimmed, shredded
75 g pistachios, toasted, coarsely chopped
1/2 C. coriander leaves
lemon wedge, to serve

Directions

1. Before you do anything preheat the oven to 400 F. Cover a baking sheet with a piece of parchment paper.
2. Lay the kumara in the baking sheet and drizzle some of the oil on it. Sprinkle some salt and pepper on it. Cook it in the oven for 22 min.
3. Bring a large saucepan of water to a boil. Add the broad beans and cook it 3 min. Drain it and rinse it with cool water. Remove the broad bean peel.
4. Place a large saucepan over medium heat. Heat the rest of the oil in it. Sauté in it the onion for 6 min.
5. Stir in the ginger, cumin, coriander, turmeric and paprika. Sauté them for 2 min.
6. Combine the stock with quinoa in a large saucepan. Cook them until they start boiling. Lower the heat and put on the lid. Cook them for 16 min.
7. Add the kale and cook them for 2 min. Stir in the kumara, broad beans and pistachios, salt and pepper. Serve your Pilaf warm.
8. Enjoy.

Persian
Noodles Bean Soup

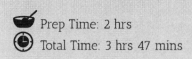

Prep Time: 2 hrs

Total Time: 3 hrs 47 mins

Servings per Recipe: 8	
Calories	414.9
Fat	23.5g
Cholesterol	2.7mg
Sodium	563.9mg
Carbohydrates	43.8g
Protein	11.7g

Ingredients

100 g chickpeas
100 g lentils
100 g navy beans or 100 g kidney beans
250 g flat wheat noodles
1/2 C. closely packed fresh coriander, finely chopped
1/2 C. closely packed fresh spinach, finely chopped
1/2 C. closely packed fresh chives, finely chopped
1/2 C. closely packed fresh dill, finely chopped (tips)
1/2 C. closely packed fresh parsley, finely chopped

1/2 C. oil
3 tbsp plain flour
1 C. buttermilk
2 tbsp sour cream
1/2 tsp turmeric
1/2 tsp ground black pepper, to taste
100 g walnuts (kernels)
1/4 C. crushed dried mint
1/2 tbsp salt, to taste
4 medium onions
6 C. water
9 C. water
1/2 C. water

Directions

1. Soak the chickpeas in some water for 2 h 30 min. Place a large pot over medium heat. Pour 6 C. of water in the pot. Add the chickpeas and cook it for 45 min.
2. Clean the lentils with some water. Stir them into the pot and cook them for 25 min while stirring often. Clean it.
3. Clean the herbs with some water and dry them.
4. Place a large pan over medium heat. Heat 1/4 C. oil in it. Chop the onion and cook in it for 6 min. Place half of it aside. Stir in the turmeric and cook them for 2 min.
5. Stir the cooked turmeric onion with 9 C. of water and noodles. Cook them for 6 min.
6. Whisk half C. of water with flour until they become smooth. Stir it with the chopped herbs into the pot. Lower the heat and cook them for 42 min.
7. Add the buttermilk with sour cream. Cook them for 3 min.

8. Heat 1/4 C. of oil in it in a large pan. Cook in it the dry mint for 2 min. Serve your soup hot with the dried mint warm.

9. Enjoy.

Persian
Lemon Chicken Kabobs

Prep Time: 10 mins

Total Time: 40 mins

Servings per Recipe: 4
Calories	432.4
Fat	33.7g
Cholesterol	92.8mg
Sodium	673.4mg
Carbohydrates	1.1g
Protein	30.3g

Ingredients

4 boneless chicken breasts, cut in cubes
6 tbsp olive oil
1/16 tsp saffron, crushed
3 tbsp lemon juice
1 tsp salt
1/4 tsp pepper
1/4 tsp basil

1/4 tsp turmeric
1/4 tsp garlic powder

Directions

1. Get a large mixing bowl: Stir into it all the ingredients. Place it in the fridge for 2 h 30 min.
2. Preheat the grill and grease its grates.
3. Thread the chicken pieces into skewers and cook them on the grill for 35 min while turning them often. Serve your kabobs warm.
4. Enjoy.

PERSIAN
Chicken Wings Soup

Prep Time: 20 mins
Total Time: 1 hr 30 mins

Servings per Recipe: 6

Calories	656.2
Fat	36.0g
Cholesterol	165.3mg
Sodium	934.2mg
Carbohydrates	34.0g
Protein	47.9g

Ingredients

1/4 C. canola oil
1 lb chicken wings
kosher salt & freshly ground black
pepper, to taste
3 medium onions (2 roughly chopped,
1 minced)
3 medium carrots, roughly chopped
2 garlic cloves, crushed
8 C. chicken stock
1 bay leaf

1 1/2 lbs ground chicken
1 1/2 C. chickpea flour
2 1/2 tsp ground turmeric
2 tsp ground coriander
1 1/2 tsp baking soda
1/2 tsp ground cardamom

Directions

1. Place a soup pot over medium heat. Heat 3 tbsp of oil in it.
2. Sprinkle some salt and pepper over the chicken wings. Brown it in the pot for 14 min. Stir in the onions, carrots, and garlic. Sauté them for 10 min.
3. Stir in the stock, bay leaf, and salt. Cook them until they start boiling. Lower the heat and cook the soup for 37 min.
4. Pour the broth in a colander and drain it. Discard the chicken wings with veggies. Pour the broth into the pot.
5. Heat the oil in a large pan. Add the onion and cook them for 5 min. Allow it to cool down slightly.
6. Get a large mixing bowl: Combine in it the rest of the ingredients and mix them well. Shape the mix into meatballs.
7. Stir the meatballs into the hot broth. Cook them until they start simmering. Put on half a cover over the pot. Cook the soup for 18 min. Serve your soup warm.
8. Enjoy.

Potato and Pepper Meatballs

🥣 Prep Time: 15 mins
🕐 Total Time: 1 hr

Servings per Recipe: 6
Calories	188.5
Fat	3.3g
Cholesterol	124.0mg
Sodium	88.8mg
Carbohydrates	32.2g
Protein	7.9g

Ingredients

5 medium potatoes or 600 g potatoes
4 eggs
1 medium green bell pepper, chopped
1/4 tsp saffron
salt

pepper
1/2 tsp baking powder
frying oil

Directions

1. Bring a salted pot of water to a boil. Cook in it the potato until it becomes soft. Drain it and place it aside.
2. Place the potato in a grater and grate it.
3. Get a large mixing bowl: Mix in it the potato with eggs, bell pepper, a pinch of salt and pepper. Mix them well. Add the saffron with baking powder. Mix them again.
4. Place a large skillet over medium heat. Heat the oil in it. Shape the mix into patties and cook them in the pan for 10 min on each side with the lid on.
5. Serve your potato patties warm.
6. Enjoy.

PERSIAN
Chicken Berries Pilaf

Prep Time: 15 mins
Total Time: 1 hr

Servings per Recipe: 4

Calories	1371.1
Fat	77.8g
Cholesterol	279.9mg
Sodium	567.0mg
Carbohydrates	129.0g
Protein	43.7g

Ingredients

7 oz. raisins
6 oz. barberries
6 onions, large
1/2 lb butter
salt, to taste

pepper, to taste
8 chicken thighs
2 C. basmati rice

Directions

1. Before you do anything preheat the oven to 400 F.
2. Place a large pan over medium heat. Heat 2 oz. of butter until it melts. Sprinkle some salt and pepper over the chicken thighs. Coat it with some of the melted butter.
3. Lay the chicken thighs on a lined up baking sheet. Cook it in the oven for 48 min.
4. Cut the onion into slices. Cook it in the pan with a pinch of salt for 4 min. Add the raisins with barberries. Cook them for 1 min. Turn off the heat and let the mix cool down slightly.
5. Put the chicken thighs on a serving plate and top them with rice and onion berries mix. Serve it warm.
6. Enjoy.

Persian
Lime Lamb Stew

Prep Time: 45 mins
Total Time: 3 hrs 15 mins

Servings per Recipe: 6
Calories	244.3
Fat	15.8g
Cholesterol	48.3mg
Sodium	493.9mg
Carbohydrates	9.0g
Protein	18.2g

Ingredients

2 large onions, peeled and thinly sliced
1 lb stew meat, cut in 1-inch cubes (lamb, veal or beef)
1/3 C. oil
1 tsp salt
1/2 tsp ground black pepper
1/2 tsp turmeric
5 stalks celery, washed and cut into 1 inch lengths
3 C. chopped fresh parsley
1/2 chopped of fresh mint
1/3 C. fresh squeezed lime juice

Directions

1. Place a pot over medium heat. Add 3 tbsp of oil and heat it. Cook in it the lamb meat with onion, turmeric, a pinch of salt and pepper. Cook them for 4 min.
2. Stir in 2 C. of water. Put on the lid and cook them for 35 min.
3. Place a large pan over medium heat. Heat 3 tbsp of oil in it. Add the celery and sauté it for 12 min. Stir in the herbs and cook them for 12 min.
4. Transfer the mix to the pot with lime juice. Put on the lid and cook them for 1 h 35 min. Adjust the seasoning of the soup then serve it warm.
5. Enjoy.

PERSIAN
Zucchini Frittata

Prep Time: 10 mins
Total Time: 55 mins

Servings per Recipe: 6
Calories	80.1
Fat	3.5g
Cholesterol	141.0mg
Sodium	160.6mg
Carbohydrates	7.2g
Protein	5.5g

Ingredients

2 medium onions, chopped
4 garlic cloves, minced
1 lb zucchini, grated
4 eggs
1/2 tsp turmeric

1/2 tsp baking soda
salt and pepper
olive oil
cooking spray

Directions

1. Place a large pan over medium heat. Heat the oil in it. Sauté in it the turmeric with onion for 3 min.
2. Add the zucchini with a pinch of salt and pepper. Cook them for 4 min.
3. Get a large mixing bowl: Beat the eggs in it. Add the baking soda with a pinch of salt and pepper. Whisk them again. Fold in the onion and zucchini mix.
4. Before you do anything preheat the oven to 375 F.
5. Pour the mix into a greased baking dish. Cook it in the oven for 35 min. Serve it warm.
6. Enjoy.

Persian
Spinach Frittata

🥣 Prep Time: 10 mins
🕐 Total Time: 30 mins

Servings per Recipe: 3
Calories	328.1
Fat	20.2g
Cholesterol	423.0mg
Sodium	769.3mg
Carbohydrates	19.2g
Protein	21.9g

Ingredients

2 lbs fresh baby spinach leaves
1/4 C. water
2 tbsp oil
2 medium onions, sliced thin (1 C.)
1/2 tsp salt (to taste)

1/8 tsp ground turmeric
1/8 tsp pepper
6 eggs

Directions

1. Pour 1/4 C. of water in a medium sauce. Pour into it 1/4 C. of water in it. Put on the lid and cook them for 6 min. Turn off the heat and let the spinach sit for 6 min.

2. Drain the spinach and squeeze it from the water.

3. Place a large pan over medium heat. Heat the oil in it. Add the onion with turmeric, a pinch of salt and pepper. Cook them for 4 min.

4. Stir in the spinach for 4 min. Make 6 holes in them. Crack an egg in each hole. Cook them for 6 min over low heat until the eggs are done. Serve your skillet warm.

5. Enjoy.

GLAZED
Lamb with Fruit Salad

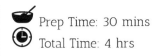 Prep Time: 30 mins

Total Time: 4 hrs

Servings per Recipe: 6
Calories	95.5
Fat	4.8g
Cholesterol	0.0mg
Sodium	10.6mg
Carbohydrates	14.4g
Protein	1.4g

Ingredients

4 tbsp pomegranate molasses
1 tsp ground cumin
1 lemon, juice of
1 tbsp olive oil
2 garlic cloves, minced
1 onion, roughly chopped
1 lamb shoulder, weighing about 1 . 6kg,
lightly scored

2 pomegranates, seeds only
handful flat leaf parsley
100 g watercress
1 small red onion, finely diced
1 tbsp olive oil
flat bread, to serve

Directions

1. Before you do anything preheat the oven to 320 F.
2. Get a small mixing bowl: Stir in it the molasses with the cumin, lemon juice, olive oil and garlic to make the sauce.
3. Spread the onion in a greased casserole dish. Place the lamb on it and pour the sauce all over it. Pour 3/4 over the lamb mix.
4. Place a large piece of foil over the casserole dish. Cook it in the oven for 3 h 30 min.
5. Toss the red onion with pomegranate and olive oil in a large salad bowl. Serve it with the roasted lamb warm.
6. Enjoy.

Persian
Creamy Dill Chicken Salad

Prep Time: 10 mins

Total Time: 1 hr 10 mins

Servings per Recipe: 6

Calories	268.4
Fat	8.4g
Cholesterol	124.7mg
Sodium	842.5mg
Carbohydrates	35.4g
Protein	13.0g

Ingredients

5 white potatoes
3 dill pickles
1 onion, halved
1 1/2 C. green peas, frozen
3 carrots, peeled
1 chicken breast
3 eggs
4 tbsp white vinegar

4 tbsp light mayonnaise
1/2 tsp turmeric
salt and pepper

Directions

1. Pour 2 C. of water in a pot and cook it until it starts boiling. Add the chicken breast, onion, carrots, turmeric, and some salt. Cook them for 50 min. Allow the mix to cool down.
2. Drain the onion and discard it. Drain the chicken and shred it. Place it aside. Dice the carrots and place them aside.
3. Combine the potato with eggs in another pot and cover them with water. Cook them for 14 min. Peel the eggs and place them aside. Peel the potatoes and dice them. Dice the pickles.
4. Get a large mixing bowl: Toss in it the potatoes, chicken, carrots, pickles, peas, and eggs.
5. Get a small mixing bowl: Mix in it the vinegar with mayonnaise, a pinch of salt and pepper. Add the mix to the veggies and chicken. Serve your salad.
6. Enjoy.

PERSIAN
Saffron Kabobs

Prep Time: 20 mins
Total Time: 40 mins

Servings per Recipe: 8
Calories   185.7
Fat   9.4g
Cholesterol   101.5mg
Sodium   387.0mg
Carbohydrates   1.9g
Protein   23.4g

Ingredients

2 lbs lean ground turkey
1 medium onion
1 egg
1 tbsp dried dill
1 tbsp dried coriander
1 tsp cumin
1 tsp sea salt
1/2 tsp pepper

1/4 tsp cayenne pepper
1/4 tsp turmeric
1/4 tsp saffron thread
1 pinch salt

Directions

1. Grate the onion in a grater. Squeeze it from the liquid.
2. Get a large mixing bowl: Toss in it the turkey, grated onion, egg, and remaining spices, except for the saffron threads.
3. Place a large pan over medium heat. Cook in it the saffron with a pinch of salt. Cook them for 10 sec. Transfer it to a mortar and grind it. Stir it into the turkey mix.
4. Mix them well. Place the mix in the fridge for an overnight.
5. Shape the mix into 8 or 10 logs and press them into the skewers. Place them in the fridge for an hour or more.
6. Preheat the oven broiler. Place the skewers on a roasting pan and cook them in the oven for 10 min on each side. Serve them warm.
7. Enjoy.

Persian
Tongues Stew

 Prep Time: 5 mins
 Total Time: 5 hrs 5 mins

Servings per Recipe: 4
Calories	232.5
Fat	20.9g
Cholesterol	53.4mg
Sodium	208.4mg
Carbohydrates	10.0g
Protein	4.9g

Ingredients

1 beef tongue
1 sheep tongue
2 - 3 garlic cloves
1 medium onion
3 - 4 tsp tomato paste
500 g mushrooms

100 g butter
200 g parsley (ends)
salt
black pepper

Directions

1. Clean the beef and sheep tongues well with cool water.
2. Place them in a large soup pot. Cover them with hot water. Cook them until foam start rising on top.
3. Slice the garlic and onion then add them to the pot. Chop the herbs and add them to the pot with some salt and peppers.
4. Cook them over low heat for 4 h 30 min. Peel the tongues and remove their skin. Slice them.
5. Place a large pan over medium heat. Melt the butter in it. Slice the mushroom and cook it in it for 4 min. Add the tomato paste with the rest of the liquid from the tongues pot.
6. Cook them until they start boiling. Keep cooking them for 3 min. Pour the mix all over the slices tongues and serve them warm.
7. Enjoy.

PERSIAN
Lentils and Meatballs Soup

Prep Time: 20 mins
Total Time: 1 hr 20 mins

Servings per Recipe: 6
Calories	145.6
Fat	6.1g
Cholesterol	31.0mg
Sodium	811.2mg
Carbohydrates	11.9g
Protein	10.6g

Ingredients

SOUP
1/4 C. lentils
1/4 C. dried black-eyed peas
4 -5 C. water
1 1/2 tsp salt
1 C. fine egg noodles
1/2 C. chopped parsley
MEATBALLS
1/2 lb ground beef
1/3 C. finely chopped onions or 1/3 C.
grated onion
1/4 tsp cinnamon

1/4 tsp fine grind black pepper
1/2 tsp salt
SPICE GARNISH
2 tsp dried mint
1/2 tsp black pepper
1/4 tsp cinnamon

Directions

1. Place a large pot of water over medium heat with a pinch of salt. Cook in it the beans with lentils for 38 min. Stir in the parsley with noodles.

2. Get a large mixing bowl: Combine in it the meatballs ingredients and mix them well. Shape the mix into meatballs. Add them to the pot and cook them for 35 min.

3. Get a mortar: Crush in it the mint with cinnamon and pepper. Sprinkle it over the soup then serve it warm.

4. Enjoy.

Persian
Eggplant Frittata

Persian

🥣 Prep Time: 15 mins

🕐 Total Time: 1 hr 25 mins

Servings per Recipe: 4

Calories	432.0
Fat	32.8g
Cholesterol	211.5mg
Sodium	766.5mg
Carbohydrates	27.5g
Protein	11.2g

Ingredients

2 large eggplants or 6 small eggplants, peeled and cut into thin strips
1 egg white, lightly beaten
1/2 C. vegetable oil, butter or 1/2 C. ghee
2 large onions, peeled and thinly sliced
4 garlic cloves, peeled and crushed
4 eggs
4 tbsp chopped fresh parsley

1/4 tsp powdered saffron, dissolved in 1 tbsp hot water
1 lime, juice of
1 tsp baking powder
1 tbsp all-purpose flour
1 tsp salt
1/4 tsp fresh ground black pepper

Directions

1. Remove the peel of the eggplants. Season them with some salt. Slice them into lengthwise. Brush both sides of the eggplant with the white egg.
2. Place a large pan over medium heat. Heat 4 tbsp of oil in it. Cook in it the onion for 12 min. Cook in it the garlic with eggplant for 12 min.
3. Before you do anything preheat the oven to 350 F.
4. Line up a baking dish with a parchment paper. Spread in the bottom of it 4 tbsp of vegetable oil.
5. Get a large mixing bowl: Whisk in it the eggs. Combine in it the parsley, saffron water, lime juice, baking powder, flour, salt, and pepper. Mix them well.
6. Combine the eggplant, onion and garlic. Stir them well. Cook them for 48 min. Serve your frittata warm.
7. Enjoy.

PERSIAN
Nutty Duck

Prep Time: 30 mins
Total Time: 1 hr 30 mins

Servings per Recipe: 4

Calories	1396.2
Fat	131.3g
Cholesterol	240.9mg
Sodium	204.6mg
Carbohydrates	13.9g
Protein	38.5g

Ingredients

1 duck, cut into quarters
2 onions, sliced
10 oz. finely chopped walnuts
2 1/2 C. water
salt and pepper, to taste

4 tbsp pomegranate syrup
2 tbsp sugar
2 tbsp lemon juice

Directions

1. Sprinkle some salt and pepper over the duck.
2. Place a large stew pot over medium heat. Melt in it the duck fat. Brown in it the duck pieces for 5 min. Add the onion and cook it for 3 min.
3. Remove the duck pieces from the pot and place them aside. Stir in the walnuts with 2 1/2 C. of water, a pinch of salt and pepper. Cook them for 1 min.
4. Stir in back the duck pieces. Cook them until they start boiling. Lower the heat and cook them for 1 h 10 min.
5. Get a small mixing bowl: Whisk in it the pomegranate syrup and sugar with the lemon juice. Spoon the fat from the rose on top and discard it.
6. Lower the heat and cook it for 32 min. Serve it warm.
7. Enjoy.

Persian
Nutty Fruit Salad

🥣 Prep Time: 5 mins
🕐 Total Time: 5 mins

Servings per Recipe: 6	
Calories	442.5
Fat	12.7g
Cholesterol	0.0mg
Sodium	82.8mg
Carbohydrates	84.2g
Protein	8.1g

Ingredients

2 seedless oranges, peeled and cored
2 apples, peeled and cored
2 bananas, sliced
2 C. pitted dates, chopped
1 C. dried figs, chopped or 1 C. apricot

1 C. orange juice
1 C. almonds, chopped or 1 C. shredded coconut

Directions

1. Get a large mixing bowl: Stir in it the oranges with apples, bananas, dates and figs.
2. Pour the orange juice all over it and mix it well. Top it with almonds then place it in the fridge until ready to serve.
3. Enjoy.

PERSIAN
Nutty Yogurt Soup

Prep Time: 10 mins
Total Time: 10 mins

Servings per Recipe: 6
Calories   110.9
Fat   5.4g
Cholesterol   21.2mg
Sodium   77.2mg
Carbohydrates   10.3g
Protein   6.2g

Ingredients

32 fluid oz. plain yogurt
1/2 C. kefir cheese
1 large cucumber
2 tbsp mint (dried and crushed)
2 tbsp basil (fresh finely chopped)
1 tsp onion powder (optional)
2 tbsp dried rose petals (optional)

1/2 C. walnuts (crushed) (optional)
1/2 C. raisins (optional)
salt
1 tbsp black pepper, to taste

Directions

1. Get a large mixing bowl: Combine in it the yogurt and kefir cheese. Mix them well.
2. Peel the cucumbers and chop them finely. Stir in the basil, mint, salt, pepper, onion powder, raisins, walnuts, and dried rose petals. Place it in the fridge until ready to serve.
3. Enjoy.

Persian
Rosy Rice Pudding

Prep Time: 2 mins
Total Time: 42 mins

Servings per Recipe: 4

Calories	1846.8
Fat	1.4g
Cholesterol	0.0mg
Sodium	5.1mg
Carbohydrates	443.9g
Protein	16.1g

Ingredients

500 g rice
1 kg sugar
cooking oil
1/2 tsp saffron
1/2 C. rose water

pistachios, crushed
almonds, crushed
1 tsp cinnamon

Directions

1. Rinse the rice with some water and drain it.
2. Place a large pot over medium heat. Place in it the rice and cover it with 6 times the amount of rice in water. Cook the rice until it is done.
3. Stir in the sugar until it completely melts.
4. Pour half C. of water in a small bowl. Stir in it the saffron then add it to the pot.
5. Pour the oil in a small saucepan. Heat it through and add it to the pot. Stir in the rosewater with almonds.
6. Lower the heat and cook the rice pudding for 30 min. Serve it warm with your favorite toppings.
7. Enjoy.

FENUGREEK
Lamb Stew

Prep Time: 20 mins
Total Time: 2 hrs 50 mins

Servings per Recipe: 6
Calories	356.9
Fat	20.4g
Cholesterol	98.4mg
Sodium	207.4mg
Carbohydrates	9.0g
Protein	33.2g

Ingredients

2 lbs boneless lamb stewing meat (cut into 3/4-inch cubes) or 2 lbs boneless beef roast (cut into 3/4-inch cubes)
1 large onion, finely chopped
1/3 C. cooking oil
1 tsp turmeric
1 1/2 C. water
6 dried limes or 1/2 C. fresh lime juice
3/4 C. kidney bean
1 large potato, diced (optional)

salt
black pepper
1 C. green onion, finely chopped
1 1/2 C. spinach, finely chopped
1/2 C. parsley, finely chopped
1/4 C. cilantro, finely chopped (optional)
1/4 C. garlic chives, finely chopped
1/4 C. fenugreek seeds, finely chopped (optional)

Directions

1. Discard the excess fat for the lamb and cut it into dices.
2. Place a large pan over medium heat. Heat in it half of the oil. Sauté in it the onion for 3 min. Add the lamb dices and cook them for 2 min.
3. Lower the heat then stir in the water, drained kidney beans, salt and pepper. Put on the lid and cook them for 1 h 10 min.
4. Place a large skillet over medium heat. Heat the rest of the oil in it. Add the potato and cook it until it becomes golden brown.
5. Drain the potato and stir it into the stew. Put on the lid and cook them for 12 min.
6. Add the remaining veggies into the same skillet and cook them for 4 min. Stir the mix with dry lime into the stew.
7. Put on the lid and cook the stew for 14 min. Serve it warm.
8. Enjoy.

Persian Cinnamon Beef Stew

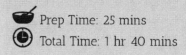

Prep Time: 25 mins
Total Time: 1 hr 40 mins

Servings per Recipe: 4
Calories   425.1
Fat   24.3g
Cholesterol   82.9mg
Sodium   388.7mg
Carbohydrates   21.3g
Protein   30.0g

Ingredients

3 tbsp olive oil, divided (2 tbsp. and 1 tbsp.)
1/2 large onion, chopped
1 lb lean stewing beef, cubed
2 tsp ground cumin
2 tsp ground turmeric
1/2 tsp ground cinnamon
2 1/2 C. water
5 tbsp fresh flat-leaf parsley, chopped
3 tbsp snipped chives

1 (15 oz.) cans kidney beans, drained and rinsed
1 lemon, juice of
1 tbsp flour
salt and black pepper

Directions

1. Place a large pan over medium heat. Heat 2 tbsp of olive oil in it. Brown in it the stew meat for 12 min.
2. Stir in the cumin, turmeric and cinnamon. Cook them for 2 min. Pour in the water and cook them until they start boiling.
3. Put on the lid and cook them for 48 min while stirring from to time.
4. Place a small skillet over medium heat. Heat 1 tbsp of oil in it. Add the parsley with chives. Cook them for 3 min. Stir them into the beef stew with beans and lemon juice.
5. Sprinkle some salt and pepper on the stew then add to it 1 tbsp of flour. Cook the stew for 35 min until it thickens. Serve it warm.
6. Enjoy.

PERSIAN
Lemon Kabobs

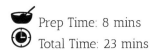

Prep Time: 8 mins
Total Time: 23 mins

Servings per Recipe: 12
Calories	94.9
Fat	5.8g
Cholesterol	25.7mg
Sodium	235.6mg
Carbohydrates	2.7g
Protein	7.4g

Ingredients

1 lb ground beef or 1 lb lamb
1 medium onion, grated
1/4 C. breadcrumbs or 1/4 C. white flour
1 egg, slightly beaten (optional)
1 tsp turmeric

1 tsp salt
1/2 tsp pepper
1 tbsp lemon juice

Directions

1. Squeeze the onion for the liquid. Transfer it to a large mixing bowl with the rest of the ingredients. Mix them well and place them in the fridge.
2. Preheat a grill and grease its grates.
3. Shape the mix into 10 or 12 patties. Press them into skewers to make logs. Cook the kabobs on the grill for 6 to 8 min on each side. Serve them warm.
4. Enjoy.

Cucumber, Onion, Parsley, and Tomato Salad (Shiraz)

Prep Time: 20 mins
Total Time: 20 mins

Servings per Recipe: 4
Calories	67.6
Fat	3.6g
Cholesterol	0.0mg
Sodium	5.5mg
Carbohydrates	9.0g
Protein	1.3g

Ingredients

1 large cucumber
1 large tomatoes
1 large onion
parsley

salt
1/4 C. lemon juice
1 - 2 tbsp olive oil

Directions

1. Chop the tomato, cucumber and onion finely.

2. In a bowl, add the chopped vegetables, the parsley, lemon juice, olive oil and salt and mix well.

PERSIAN
Meat and Kidney Bean Stew (Khoresh)

 Prep Time: 25 mins

🕐 Total Time: 1 hr 40 mins

Servings per Recipe: 4
Calories	425.1
Fat	24.3g
Cholesterol	82.9mg
Sodium	388.7mg
Carbohydrates	21.3g
Protein	30.0g

Ingredients

3 tbsp olive oil, divided
1/2 large onion, chopped
1 lb. lean stewing beef, cubed
2 tsp ground cumin
2 tsp ground turmeric
1/2 tsp ground cinnamon
2 1/2 C. water
5 tbsp fresh flat-leaf parsley, chopped
3 tbsp snipped chives

1 (15 oz.) cans kidney beans, drained and rinsed
1 lemon, juice of
1 tbsp flour
salt and black pepper

Directions

1. In a large pan, heat 2 tbsp of the oil and sauté the onion till golden.
2. Add the stewing beef and cook for about 10 minutes.
3. Add the cumin, turmeric and cinnamon and cook for about 1 minute, stirring continuously.
4. Add the water and bring to a boil.
5. Reduce the heat to low and simmer, covered for about 45 minutes, stirring occasionally.
6. In a small frying pan, heat the remaining 1 tbsp of the oil and sauté the parsley and chives for about 2 minutes.
7. In the pan of the beef, add the parsley mixture, kidney beans, lemon juice, salt and pepper and stir to combine.
8. In a small bowl, mix together 1 tbsp of the flour and a bit of hot water.
9. Add the flour mixture into the beef mixture, stirring continuously and simmer, uncovered for about 30 minutes.

National
Iranian Green Stew

🥣 Prep Time: 20 mins
🕐 Total Time: 2 hrs 50 mins

Servings per Recipe: 6
Calories	356.9
Fat	20.4g
Cholesterol	98.4mg
Sodium	207.4mg
Carbohydrates	9.0g
Protein	33.2g

Ingredients

2 lb. boneless lamb stewing meat
1 large onion, finely chopped
1/3 C. cooking oil
1 tsp turmeric
1 1/2 C. water
1/2 C. fresh lime juice
3/4 C. kidney bean (canned is fine)
1 large potato, diced
salt
black pepper

1 C. green onion, finely chopped
1 1/2 C. spinach, finely chopped
1/2 C. parsley, finely chopped
1/4 C. cilantro, finely chopped
1/4 C. garlic chives, finely chopped (tareh)
1/4 C. fenugreek seeds, finely chopped

Directions

1. Trim the lamb meat and cut into 3/4-inch cubes.
2. In a large pan, heat 3 tbsp of the oil on medium heat and sauté the onion ill golden.
3. Add turmeric and sauté for about 2 minutes.
4. Stir in the meat cubes and increase the heat to high.
5. Sear the meat till browned completely.
6. Add the water, kidney beans, salt and pepper and stir to combine.
7. Reduce the heat and simmer, covered for about 1 hour.
8. In a skillet, heat the remaining oil on high heat and fry the potatoes till lightly browned.
9. With a slotted spoon, transfer the potatoes into the meat mixture, leaving oil in the skillet.
10. Simmer, covered for about 10 minutes.
11. In the skillet, add prepared vegetables on medium heat and fry till wilted.
12. Transfer the vegetables into the meat mixture with the lime juice and simmer, covered for about 10-15 minutes.

HOW TO MAKE
Authentic Rice from Persia

Prep Time: 25 mins
Total Time: 1 hr 10 mins

Servings per Recipe: 8
Calories   311.5
Fat   11.8g
Cholesterol   30.5mg
Sodium   408.1mg
Carbohydrates   46.2g
Protein   4.4g

Ingredients

2 C. long grain rice, washed
1 tsp salt
2 potatoes, peeled and very thinly sliced

12 C. cold water
1/2 C. melted butter

Directions

1. In a large pan of the lightly salted boiling water, cook the rice for about 10 minutes.
2. Drain the rice and reserve in a bowl.
3. Coat the potato slices with the melted butter evenly.
4. In the bottom of the same pan, arrange the potato slices and top with the leftover butter from the bottom of the bowl.
5. Carefully, place the cooked rice over the potato slices.
6. Cover the pot with a tea towel and then with its lid tightly.
7. Place the pan on medium-low heat and cook for about 1/2 hour.
8. Remove from the heat and carefully, invert over a large platter.
9. Serve immediately.

Nutty Persian Pomegranate Chicken (Fesenjan)

🍳 Prep Time: 20 mins
🕐 Total Time: 1 hr

Servings per Recipe: 4	
Calories	1176.3
Fat	93.5g
Cholesterol	245.8mg
Sodium	432.1mg
Carbohydrates	23.9g
Protein	64.7g

Ingredients

1/4 C. lime juice
1/4 C. butter
2 1/2-3 lb. chicken (cut up, bone-in)
2 onions, thinly sliced
2 C. walnuts, finely ground in a food processor
1 1/2-2 C. chicken stock
2/3 C. pomegranate syrup
2 -3 tbsp sugar
kosher salt, to taste
fresh ground pepper, to taste

Directions

1. Drizzle the chicken pieces with the lime juice evenly and refrigerate to marinate for about 1-4 hours.
2. In a large, heavy-bottomed pan, melt 2 tbsp of the butter on medium heat and cook the chicken pieces in batches till browned from all sides.
3. Transfer the chicken pieces into a plate.
4. In the same pan, melt the remaining butter and sauté the onions till translucent.
5. Stir in the ground walnuts and sauté for about 30 seconds.
6. Add the stock and cooked chicken pieces and bring to a boil.
7. Reduce the heat and simmer, covered for about 20-30 minutes.
8. Stir in the pomegranate juice, sugar, salt and pepper and simmer for about 15-20 minutes.
9. Serve hot.

TRADITIONAL
Persian Pilaf and Lentils

Prep Time: 10 mins
Total Time: 1 hr 10 mins

Servings per Recipe: 4
Calories	747.5
Fat	14.9g
Cholesterol	30.5mg
Sodium	702.8mg
Carbohydrates	141.8g
Protein	17.2g

Ingredients

1 1/2 C. lentils, soaked
2 C. basmati rice
2 C. water
1 onion, sliced thinly
3 garlic cloves, minced
1 tsp salt
1/4 tsp pepper
1/2 tsp turmeric
1/4 tsp cinnamon
1/8 tsp nutmeg

1/4 tsp cardamom
1/8 tsp cumin
1/2 tsp saffron, dissolved in 2 tbsp water
3/4 C. raisins
3/4 C. dates, pitted and chopped
1 potato, sliced into thin rounds
canola oil
1/4 C. butter, melted

Directions

1. In a large pan of the salted boiling water, cook the lentils on low heat for about 20-30 minutes.
2. Drain water from lentils and keep aside.
3. In another pan, heat the oil and sauté the onions and garlic till tender.
4. Stir in the raisins, dates, and spices except saffron and remove from the heat.
5. Rinse the rice under cold water completely.
6. In a rice cooker, add the rice, 2 C. of the water, 1/2 tsp of the salt and a drizzle of the oil and cook till done completely.
7. Transfer the cooked rice into a large bowl.
8. In the rice cooker, add enough oil to just cover the bottom surface.
9. In the bottom of the rice cooker, arrange the potato slices, followed by a layer of the rice, a layer of the lentil mixture.
10. Repeat the layers, ending with a layer of the rice.
11. Cover and press the "Cook" button and cook for about 10 minutes.

12. Drizzle melted butter and saffron water over the rice and cover with a tea towel and seal with the lid.

13. Cook for about 30 minutes.

ALTERNATIVE
Citrus and Ginger Persian Pilaf

Prep Time: 10 mins
Total Time: 35 mins

Servings per Recipe: 6
Calories	311.2
Fat	7.7g
Cholesterol	10.1mg
Sodium	692.9mg
Carbohydrates	54.8g
Protein	6.6g

Ingredients

2 tbsp butter
1 1/3 C. uncooked rice
1 tsp salt
3/4 C. raisins
1/8-1/4 tsp red pepper flakes
1 inch piece ginger root, minced
2 C. chicken broth

1 C. orange juice
1 tbsp fresh parsley
1 tbsp grated orange zest
1/4 C. almonds (toasted)

Directions

1. In a medium pan, melt the butter on medium heat and cook the rice till lightly browned, stirring continuously.
2. Add the salt, raisins, red pepper flakes, grated ginger root, chicken broth and orange juice and bring to a boil.
3. Reduce the heat and simmer, covered for about 20 minutes.
4. Remove from the heat and keep aside for about 5 minutes.
5. Stir in the parsley, orange zest and toasted almonds and serve.

How to Make
Persian Couscous with Apricots

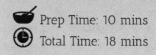 Prep Time: 10 mins

Total Time: 18 mins

Servings per Recipe: 3

Calories	419.4
Fat	14.1g
Cholesterol	20.3mg
Sodium	121.3mg
Carbohydrates	64.2g
Protein	10.9g

Ingredients

1 C. couscous
2 tsp vegetable stock powder
1/2 tsp sugar
1/2 grated an orange, rind of
2 C. boiling water
1/4-1/2 C. chopped almonds
1/4-1/2 C. currants

2 tbsp butter
1/4-1/2 C. dried apricot, chopped
2 spring onions
1/4 C. chopped coriander leaves

Directions

1. In a bowl, mix together the couscous, stock powder, sugar and grated orange rind.
2. Add the boiling water and keep aside, covered for about 6 minutes.
3. In a small frying pan, melt the butter and cook the nuts and currants till browned lightly.
4. Stir in the chopped apricots.
5. Add the hot nut mixture into the couscous and stir to combine.
6. Stir in the spring onions and coriander and serve immediately.

SPICY
Persian Bean Bowl

Prep Time: 5 mins
Total Time: 25 mins

Servings per Recipe: 4
Calories   298.4
Fat   5.2g
Cholesterol   0.0mg
Sodium   860.0mg
Carbohydrates   49.7g
Protein   15.4g

Ingredients

4 C. cooked kidney beans
1 onion
1 garlic
1/2 tsp cumin
1 dash cinnamon
1 lime, juice of
3 tbsp tomato paste

1 C. water
1 tbsp oil
1 small chili pepper
salt
pepper

Directions

1. In a large pan, heat the oil and sauté the onion till tender.
2. Add the garlic, cumin, cinnamon, lime juice, tomato paste and water and simmer for about 5 minutes.
3. Add the beans and the chili pepper and simmer for about 10 minutes.

Persian
Rose Cookies

Prep Time: 35 mins
Total Time: 57 mins

Servings per Recipe: 3
Calories	120.1
Fat	4.3g
Cholesterol	18.6mg
Sodium	11.7mg
Carbohydrates	18.3g
Protein	1.6g

Ingredients

1/3 C. canola oil
2/3 C. confectioners' sugar
2 eggs
2 tbsp Iranian rose water
2 1/4 C. rice flour

1/4 tsp baking powder
3/4 tsp ground cardamom
ground roasted pistachio nuts

Directions

1. In a bowl, mix together the canola oil and white sugar.
2. In another small bowl, beat the eggs.
3. Add the beaten eggs, rose water, white rice flour, baking powder and cardamom into the sugar mixture and mix till a thick dough is formed.
4. Refrigerate for at least 20 minutes.
5. Set your oven to 350 degrees F and line a cookie sheet with a baking paper.
6. With a spoonful of the dough roll into walnut sized balls between and with the palm of your hands, flatten slightly.
7. Arrange the cookies onto the prepared cookie sheet about 1-inch apart and sprinkle with the ground pistachios.
8. Cook in the oven for about 15-22 minutes.
9. Remove from the oven and keep onto the wire rack to cool in the pan for about 5 minutes.
10. Carefully, invert the cookies onto the wire rack to cool completely.
11. These cookies can be stored in an airtight container.

TRADITIONAL
Iranian Flat Bread

Prep Time: 2 hrs
Total Time: 2 hrs 30 mins

Servings per Recipe: 12
Calories   136.5
Fat   0.5g
Cholesterol   0.0mg
Sodium   332.4mg
Carbohydrates   28.0g
Protein   4.7g

Ingredients

3 1/4 C. bread flour
1 1/2 C. water
1 tsp baking powder
1 1/4 oz. active dry yeast
1 -1 1/2 tsp salt
2 tsp sugar
cornmeal (for bottom of pan)
poppy seeds or sesame seeds

FOR GLAZE
1 tsp flour
1 tsp baking soda
2/3 C. water

Directions

1. In a bowl, dissolve the yeast and sugar in 1/2 C. of the water and keep aside for a few minutes.
2. In a large bowl, mix together the bread flour, baking powder and salt.
3. Make a well in the center of the flour mixture.
4. Slowly, add the yeast mixture in the well and mix well.
5. Add remaining 1 C. of the water and mix till a dough is formed.
6. Place the dough onto a lightly floured surface and knead till smooth and elastic.
7. Divide the dough into 2 equal sized round pieces.
8. Sprinkle a large baking sheet with the cornmeal.
9. Arrange the dough onto the prepared baking sheet.
10. Cover the baking sheet lightly and place in a warm place for about 1 1/2 hours.
11. Set your oven to 375 degrees F.
12. Meanwhile in a pan, add the glaze ingredients and bring to a boil.
13. Remove from the heat and keep aside to cool.
14. Coat the dough portions with the glaze slightly.

15. Dip your fingers in the glaze and with the edges of your hands, punch the dough down to form several long parallel ridges along the dough.

16. Again, coat the dough portions with the glaze and sprinkle with the sesame seeds.

17. Carefully stretch each dough portion dough into 8-inch wide, 18-inch long and 1/4-1/2-inch thick breads.

18. Cook in the oven for about 25-30 minutes.

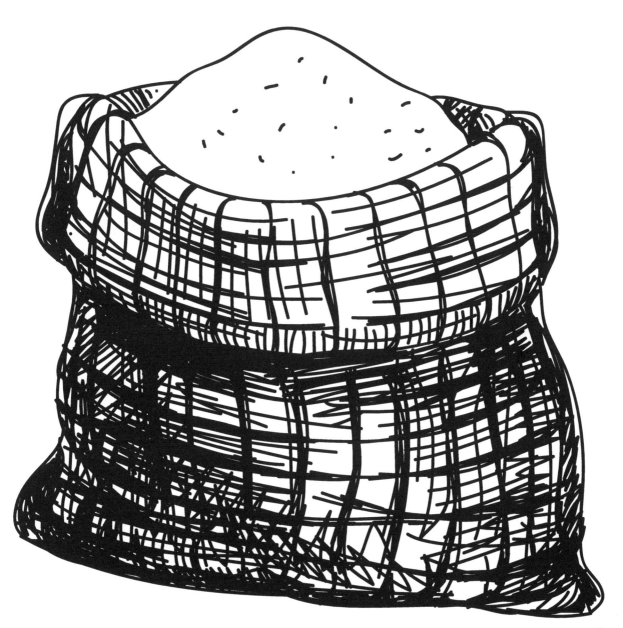

PERSIAN
Traditional Split Pea Soup

 Prep Time: 15 mins

Total Time: 1 hr 45 mins

Servings per Recipe: 4
Calories	360.3
Fat	1.5g
Cholesterol	0.0mg
Sodium	924.5mg
Carbohydrates	72.0g
Protein	18.2g

Ingredients

1/2 C. raw barley
1 bay leaf
1 garlic clove
4 C. water
1 C. dried split yellow peas
1/2 tsp cinnamon
1 tsp ground cardamom
1 C. onion, chopped
1 C. carrot, peeled and cut in 1 inch chunks

2 C. potatoes, cut in 1 inch chunks
1 1/2 tsp salt
1 pinch cayenne
2 C. vegetable broth
2 C. tomatoes, coarsely chopped
1/4 C. fresh parsley, chopped
1 lemon, juice of
salt and pepper

Directions

1. In a medium pan, add the barley, bay leaf, garlic and 2 C. of the water and bring to a boil.
2. Reduce the heat and simmer, covered for about 15 minutes.
3. Add the split peas, cardamom, cinnamon and the remaining water and simmer, covered for about 45 minutes, stirring occasionally.
4. Meanwhile in a large pan, add the onions, carrots, potatoes, salt, cayenne and stock and bring to a boil.
5. Reduce the heat and simmer, covered for about 10 minutes.
6. Stir in the tomatoes and simmer, covered for about 10 minutes.
7. Stir in the cooked barley, split peas, parsley, lemon juice, salt and pepper and remove from the heat.
8. Discard the bay leaf before serving.

Middle-Eastern Inspired Kabobs

🥣 Prep Time: 40 mins
🕐 Total Time: 1 hr

Servings per Recipe: 2
Calories   766.5
Fat   68.0g
Cholesterol   92.8mg
Sodium   97.4mg
Carbohydrates   9.4g
Protein   31.5g

Ingredients

1/2 large onion, coarsely chopped
1/4 C. fresh lemon juice
1 tbsp dried oregano
1 tbsp sweet paprika
2 garlic cloves, crushed
1/2 C. extra virgin olive oil
2 chicken breasts, cut into pieces

2 - 5 skewers, soaked in water for at least 30 minutes

Directions

1. In a small food processor, add the onion, lemon juice, oregano, paprika and garlic and pulse till pureed.
2. Add the olive oil and pulse till well combined.
3. In a large bowl, mix together the chicken and marinade and refrigerate for at least 30 minutes, flipping occasionally.
4. Set your grill for medium heat and lightly, grease the grill grate.
5. Thread the chicken pieces onto skewers and cook on grill over the direct heat for about 8 minutes per side.

MASHED
Persian Eggplant Appetizer

 Prep Time: 10 mins

Total Time: 50 mins

Servings per Recipe: 8
Calories   48.4
Fat   1.4g
Cholesterol   2.7mg
Sodium   303.2mg
Carbohydrates   8.2g
Protein   2.0g

Ingredients

2 (1 lb.) large eggplants
1 tsp olive oil
4 cloves garlic, peeled and crushed
1 tsp salt
1/2 tsp fresh ground black pepper
2/3 C. drained yogurt
4 tsp of fresh mint, chopped
2 tsp fresh lime juice
GARNISH
1/4 tsp powdered saffron, threads in

2 tsp hot water
1 tsp drained yogurt
fresh mint leaves

Directions

1. Set your oven to 350 degrees F before doing anything else.
2. Rinse the eggplants and with a fork, prick them.
3. Cook the eggplant in the oven for about 40 minutes, flipping occasionally.
4. Remove from the oven and place onto a cutting board to cool slightly.
5. Remove the skin of the eggplants and chop the flesh.
6. In a bowl, add the eggplant flesh and remaining ingredients and mix well.
7. Serve with a garnishing of the saffron water, yogurt and mint leaves.

Persian
Crock Pot Dinner

Prep Time: 30 mins
Total Time: 6 hrs 30 mins

Servings per Recipe: 4
Calories	236.3
Fat	11.6g
Cholesterol	71.4mg
Sodium	236.8mg
Carbohydrates	12.2g
Protein	20.1g

Ingredients

8 skinless chicken thighs
2 tbsp all-purpose flour
2 tsp turmeric
2 tsp paprika
2 tbsp olive oil
1 large onion, chopped
2 garlic cloves, chopped

4 cloves
1 inch piece fresh ginger, finely chopped
450 ml chicken stock
pepper

Directions

1. With a sharp knife, make deep slits in each chicken piece 2-3 times.
2. In a small plastic bag, add the chicken pieces, flour, turmeric and paprika and shake to coat slightly.
3. In a frying pan, heat the oil and cook the chicken pieces till browned from all sides.
4. Transfer the chicken pieces into a plate.
5. In the same pan, add the onion and garlic and sauté for about 5 minutes.
6. Stir in the remaining spiced flour, cloves, ginger and some pepper.
7. Slowly, add the stock, stirring continuously.
8. Bring to a boil, stirring continuously.
9. Transfer the chicken pieces into the slow cooker and top with the hot stock mixture.
10. Set the slow cooker on High and cook, covered for about 2 hours.
11. Now, set the slow cooker on Medium and cook, covered for about 4 hours

SWEET
Chicken Leg Peach Stew from Persia

🥘 Prep Time: 5 mins

🕐 Total Time: 1 hr 5 mins

Servings per Recipe: 4

Calories	551.7
Fat	27.8g
Cholesterol	141.3mg
Sodium	144.8mg
Carbohydrates	44.3g
Protein	32.5g

Ingredients

1 1/2 lb. chicken legs
1 large onion, thinly sliced into rings
2 tbsp olive oil
1/8 tsp turmeric
1/4 tsp paprika
2 - 3 tsp rose water
1/2 tsp ground cardamom
1/4 tsp cumin
1/2 tsp cinnamon
1/2 C. lime juice

1/2 C. brown sugar
3 firm peaches
1/4 tsp saffron, dissolved in hot water

Directions

1. Trim the fat and skin from the chicken and chop into bite-sized pieces.
2. Heat a nonstick pan on medium heat and cook the chicken pieces till lightly browned.
3. Add the olive oil and onions and cook till the onion becomes translucent.
4. Add the rosewater, cardamom, cumin, cinnamon and salt, pepper and 1 C. of the water and stir to combine.
5. Reduce the heat to low and simmer, covered for about 30 minutes, stirring occasionally.
6. Stir in the lime juice, sugar and simmer, covered for about 30 - 45 minutes.
7. Wash the peaches completely.
8. Remove the pits and cut into small wedges.
9. Carefully stir the peaches into the chicken and simmer, covered for about 20 - 30 minutes.
10. Serve hot.

Traditional
Persian Savory Rose Spice Mix (Advieh)

Prep Time: 2 mins
Total Time: 2 mins

Servings per Recipe: 1
Calories	28.1
Fat	1.2g
Cholesterol	0.0mg
Sodium	2.7mg
Carbohydrates	5.0g
Protein	0.6g

Ingredients

1 teaspoon ground cinnamon
1 teaspoon ground nutmeg
1 teaspoon ground rose petal

1 teaspoon ground cardamom
1/2 teaspoon ground cumin

Directions

1. Add the following to a mortar and pestle: cumin, cardamom, rose petals, nutmeg, and cinnamon.
2. Mash the ingredients together until everything is finely ground.
3. Pour your spice mix into a container for storage.
4. Enjoy.

PERSIAN
Buttery Berry Pilaf

Prep Time: 1 hr
Total Time: 2 hrs 10 mins

Servings per Recipe: 2
Calories	666.4
Fat	29.3g
Cholesterol	76.3mg
Sodium	255.0mg
Carbohydrates	93.1g
Protein	6.7g

Ingredients

1 C. rice
water
1/2 C. dried barberries
2 1/2 tbsp white sugar
2 tbsp saffron water

5 tbsp butter, divided
1/8 tsp advieh Persian mixed spice
sea salt, to taste

Directions

1. Wash the rice several times till the water runs clear.
2. In a bowl of the salted water, soak the rice for at least 1 hour.
3. Drain the rice completely.
4. In a large pan of the salted boiling water, add the rice and bring to a boil.
5. Cook for about 10 minutes.
6. Gently scoop the rice from the bottom of the pan and bring to the surface and release several times during cooking.
7. Drain the rice in a colander and rinse with cold water to stop the cooking process.
8. Pick over the barberries and remove any stones.
9. In a bowl of the water, soak the barberries for about 5-10 minutes.
10. Drain the barberries and rinse under cold water.
11. In a skillet melt 1 tbsp of the butter and cook the barberries, sugar and stir to combine well.
12. Add 1 tbsp of the saffron water and cook for about 1 minute.
13. Remove from the heat.
14. Reserve 1/4 of a C. of barberries in a bowl for the garnishing.
15. In a heavy pan, melt the remaining butter.
16. Add 1/2 tbsp of the saffron water and a couple large spoons of rice and stir to combine.

17. Sprinkle the advieh and place some barberry mixture on top.
18. Repeat the layers, ending with the rice.
19. With a spoon, make 3-4 holes in the rice.
20. Place the pan on medium-high heat and cook, covered for about 10 minutes.
21. In a small frying pan, melt 1 tbsp of the butter.
22. Add 1/2 tbsp of the saffron water and 1 tbsp of the water and mix well.
23. Place the butter mixture over the rice evenly.
24. Reduce the heat to low and cook, covered for about 1 hour.
25. Serve with a garnishing of the reserved barberries.

PERSIAN STYLE
Burgers

Prep Time: 10 mins
Total Time: 20 mins

Servings per Recipe: 6
Calories   307.9
Fat   19.2g
Cholesterol   139.1mg
Sodium   492.9mg
Carbohydrates   6.8g
Protein   25.2g

Ingredients

1 1/2 lb. ground beef
1 onion, diced
1 tbsp parsley, minced
1 tbsp cilantro, minced
1 tsp lemon zest
1 tsp cumin
1 tsp salt

1 tsp pepper
1/2 tsp turmeric
1/2 C. chickpea flour
2 eggs

Directions

1. In a bowl, add all the ingredients except the oil and mix well.

2. Make patties from the mixture.

3. In a skillet, heat the oil and cook the patties till cooked through from both sides.

Pomegranate
Persian Inspired Tacos

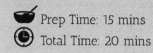 Prep Time: 15 mins

Total Time: 20 mins

Servings per Recipe: 3
Calories	512.6
Fat	33.0g
Cholesterol	102.8mg
Sodium	121.8mg
Carbohydrates	22.3g
Protein	30.9g

Ingredients

6 - 8 corn tortillas (5 inch)
GARNISH:
fresh Baby Spinach
tomatoes, diced small
lime slice
yellow hot chili pepper
green onion, thinly sliced
red onion, diced small
cucumber, diced small
avocado, diced small
fresh cilantro
fresh basil
of fresh mint
plain yogurt, drained
MEAT:
2 tbsp olive oil
1 lb. ground beef
1 garlic clove, peeled and finely minced
salt or pepper
1 - 2 tbsp pomegranate molasses
1 - 2 tsp sumac
1/2 lime, juice of

Directions

1. In a large skillet, heat the olive oil on medium heat and cook the ground beef till slightly browned.
2. Add the garlic and cook for about 5 minutes.
3. Remove skillet from the heat and stir in the salt, pepper, 1 tbsp of the pomegranate molasses and 1 tsp of the sumac.
4. Serve warm with the corn tortillas and platter of the garnishes.

MIDDLE-EASTERN
Mint Cucumber Dip (Maast-O-Khiar)

 Prep Time: 15 mins

Total Time: 15 mins

Servings per Recipe: 4
Calories   80.9
Fat   4.0g
Cholesterol   15.9mg
Sodium   57.4mg
Carbohydrates   7.2g
Protein   4.5g

Ingredients

16 oz. plain yogurt (Greek)
1/2 small cucumber, grated
one small onion, peeled and grated
2 tsp mint

salt, to taste
1/8 tsp black pepper

Directions

1. In a large bowl, add the yogurt and beat till smooth.
2. Add remaining ingredients and mix well.
3. Refrigerate for about 2 hours before serving.

Roast Beef Squash and Onion Couscous

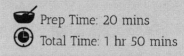

Prep Time: 20 mins
Total Time: 1 hr 50 mins

Servings per Recipe: 4
Calories   474.4
Fat   8.8g
Cholesterol   74.8mg
Sodium   884.9mg
Carbohydrates   70.1g
Protein   32.4g

Ingredients

1 tbsp vegetable oil
1 lb. boneless beef roast, in 3/4 inch chunks
1/2 tsp salt
1/8 tsp pepper
2 1/4 C. beef stock
1 1/2 tsp cinnamon
8 oz. white pearl onions, peeled

8 oz. butternut squash, in 1/2 inch cubes
3 tbsp vinegar
1 tbsp honey
1 C. pitted prune
3/4 C. couscous

Directions

1. Season the beef with the salt and pepper evenly.
2. In a pan, heat the oil on medium heat and sear the beef for about 5-8 minutes.
3. Stir in the stock and cinnamon and bring to boil.
4. Reduce the heat and simmer for about 1 hour.
5. Stir in the onions, squash, vinegar and honey and again bring to a boil.
6. Reduce the heat to low and simmer, covered for about 30 minutes.
7. Meanwhile in another pan, cook the couscous according to package's directions.
8. Add the prunes and chickpeas into the stew and cook, covered for about 2 minutes.
9. Serve the stew over the couscous.

POMEGRANATE
and Tarragon Spicy Meatballs

Prep Time: 12 mins
Total Time: 27 mins

Servings per Recipe: 1
Calories   232.2
Fat   17.8g
Cholesterol   35.3mg
Sodium   233.4mg
Carbohydrates   9.9g
Protein   9.5g

Ingredients

MEATBALLS
1 small onion, completely chopped
1 1/2 C. raw pistachios
1/4 C. breadcrumbs
2 C. fresh parsley, chopped
1 C. fresh tarragon, chopped
1 C. fresh cilantro, chopped
1 tbsp fresh lime juice
1 tsp red pepper flakes
1 tsp fresh ground black pepper
1 tbsp ground cumin
1 tsp salt
2 lb. ground lamb
1 egg
1/2 C. canola oil
GLAZE
3/4 C. pomegranate molasses
1/4 C. honey
1 tsp salt
1/2 tsp fresh ground black pepper
1/2 tsp red pepper flakes
FOR THE GARNISH
2 tbsp chopped pistachios
1 sprig basil
mixed sprouts
mint
1 C. fresh pomegranate

Directions

1. For the meatballs in a food processor, add all the ingredients, except the meat and egg and pulse till a grainy paste is formed.
2. Transfer the mixture into a large bowl.
3. Add the meat and egg and with your hands, knead lightly for a few minutes.
4. Refrigerate, covered for about 30 minutes and up to 24 hours.
5. Set your oven to 500 degrees F and generously, grease a wide, nonreactive baking dish.
6. Make bite-sized balls from the meat mixture and arrange onto the prepared baking dish.
7. Coat the balls with the oil completely and cook in the oven for about 10 minutes.
8. Meanwhile for the glaze in a bowl, mix together all the ingredients.
9. Now, set your the oven to 400 degrees F.
10. Coat the meatballs with the glaze evenly and cook in the oven for about 5 minutes.
11. Serve the meatballs with the pan sauce.

Full Persian Dinner Long Grain Rice and Chicken

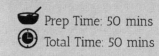

Prep Time: 50 mins

Total Time: 50 mins

Servings per Recipe: 3

Calories	1381.3
Fat	67.1g
Cholesterol	303.8mg
Sodium	2019.6mg
Carbohydrates	105.1g
Protein	84.6g

Ingredients

2 tbsp butter
1 (2 1/2-3 lb.) chicken, cut into 8 pieces
1 medium onion, chopped
1/2 C. chopped dried apricot
1/3 C. raisins
2 (14 1/2 oz.) cans chicken broth
1 tsp salt
1/4 tsp pepper

1/4 tsp ground cinnamon
1 1/2 C. uncooked long-grain rice

Directions

1. In a large pan, melt the butter and cook the chicken for about 15 minutes.
2. Transfer the chicken into a platter.
3. In the same pan, add the onion, apricots, and raisins on medium heat and sauté for about 2-3 minutes.
4. Add the chicken broth, salt, pepper and cinnamon and bring to a boil.
5. Add the rice and chicken and stir to combine.
6. Reduce the heat to low and simmer, covered for about 25 minutes.

TRADITIONAL
Lamb Stew

 Prep Time: 15 mins

Total Time: 1 hr 45 mins

Servings per Recipe: 4
Calories	280.5
Fat	8.1g
Cholesterol	72.7mg
Sodium	478.1mg
Carbohydrates	19.6g
Protein	32.1g

Ingredients

1 lb. lean lamb, cut into bite-size pieces
3 whole dried limes
3 garlic cloves, peeled
4 C. water
1 bunch cilantro, stems removed
1 bunch Italian parsley, stems removed
1 bunch mint, stems removed
1 bunch spinach, stems removed
1 bunch mustard greens, stems removed

1 (15 oz.) cans kidney beans, drained and rinsed
1/4 tsp ground cinnamon
1 pinch nutmeg
salt and pepper

Directions

1. In a large pan, add the lamb, whole dried limes, garlic and water and simmer for about 1 hour, skimming the foam from the top occasionally.
2. Meanwhile, wash all the greens completely and drain in a colander.
3. Strain the lamb stock and skim off any fat from the top.
4. Place the lamb and dried limes in a bowl and keep aside.
5. In the same pan, add the stock and bring to a boil.
6. Add the greens and simmer till wilted completely.
7. Remove from the heat and keep aside to cool.
8. In a food processor, add the greens and pulse till pureed.
9. Return the greens into the pan with the lamb, limes, kidney beans, cinnamon and nutmeg and bring to a boil.
10. Simmer for about 10-15 minutes.
11. Stir in the salt and pepper and remove from the heat.
12. Discard the limes and serve alongside the steamed white basmati rice.

Slow Cooker
Lamb Dinner

🥣 Prep Time:15 mins
🕐 Total Time: 5 hrs 15 mins

Servings per Recipe: 4
Calories   512.7
Fat   20.5g
Cholesterol   107.1mg
Sodium   453.5mg
Carbohydrates   43.2g
Protein   41.7g

Ingredients

1 1/2 lb. lean boneless leg of lamb, cut into 1 inch cubes
1/2 tsp salt
pepper
3 tbsp olive oil (divided)
2 large onions, thinly sliced
6 garlic cloves, minced
1/2 tsp dried oregano
1 (14 oz.) cans whole tomatoes, drained
1 large potato, peeled and cut into 1/2 inch cubes

8 oz. fresh green beans
1 small eggplant, peeled and cut into 1/2 inch cubes
1 medium zucchini, cut into 1/2 inch slices
5 bay leaves
3 tbsp fresh parsley, chopped

Directions

1. Season the lamb with half of the salt and pepper.
2. In a skillet, heat 2 tbsp of the oil on medium-high heat and sear the lamb till browned.
3. Transfer the lamb into a 3 1/2 quart crock pot.
4. In the same skillet, heat the remaining oil and sauté the onions for about 3-5 minutes.
5. Add the garlic and oregano and sauté for about 1 minute.
6. Add the tomatoes and simmer, smashing the tomatoes with the back of the spoon.
7. Place half of the tomatoes over the lamb in the crock pot, followed by potatoes in a layer and sprinkle with the salt and pepper.
8. Place a layer of the green beans, followed by the eggplant and zucchini and sprinkle each layer with the salt and pepper slightly.
9. Top with the remaining tomatoes and bay leaves.
10. Set the crock pot on High and cook, covered for about 4 hours.
11. Discard the bay leaves before serving.

Made in United States
Troutdale, OR
03/30/2025

30170297R00033